WITHDRAW

Contents

Prologue:
Staring at the Sea

Christopher Columbus sat on the edge of the dock and stared out across the sea. Below his feet water surged and gurgled. Towards the horizon the Mediterranean Sea was as blue as the summer sky. A breeze stirred the ten-year-old boy's sandy hair and filled the loose sails of great wooden ships, making them bump against the dock. Behind him was the tall Torra della Lanterna, Genoa's great lighthouse, which, when evening fell, would burn a huge lamp of olive oil to guide ships safely into the port.

"Out of the way, boy!"

A tanned and bearded sailor with a gold ring in his ear aimed a friendly kick at Christopher's backside. A ship had just arrived and the crew were busy unloading a cargo of cloth from Flanders.

Christopher dodged the kick and grinned up at the seaman.

The port was Christopher's favourite place. As long as he could remember he had loved the cries of the white gulls as they dived for fish and scraps, the creaking timbers and booming sails of the great ships, the sight of sailors climbing the ropes and rigging as if they were monkeys, and the smells of the ships and the sea. He loved listening to the rough – and usually rude – shouts of seamen glad to be back in port after a long voyage, or getting ready to set off for their next destination, and he loved that when he was here he felt as if he was at the centre of the world.

At the great, bustling port of Genoa, in the north of Italy, ships arrived from and sailed to many other harbours around the Mediterranean Sea, and further away. Some sailed out through the narrow Straits of Gibraltar between Spain and North Africa, onto the endless Atlantic Ocean, then north up the coasts of Spain, Portugal, and France to England or south down the western coast of mysterious Africa. To the young boy it seemed that the sailors who crowded the port had been everywhere and seen everything. The sailors always had news from other parts of the world. He heard about explorers in Africa, sea battles with pirates, and maps that were becoming ever larger as brave ships sailed to places that no one had seen before.

At the port of Genoa, the whole world seemed to be buzzing with excitement.

Christopher longed to be on one of the ships leaving the harbour, preferably one going to far distant shores. He dreamed of being one of those famous men whose adventures were known far and wide.

His family had agreed to let him go to sea when he was fourteen. In the meantime, Christopher was learning to read and write in the old language of Latin and already knew his numbers. Over the next few years he would be taught a little about drawing, maps, geography and how to use the sun and stars to find a direction. His father had also spoken with one of his cousins, a well-known sailor called Colombo. Colombo had agreed that when the time came, he would take Christopher on board his own ship.

LIVESinACTION

The year was 1461. The ten-year-old boy, who was called Cristoforo Colombo in Italian, and who would become the most famous seafarer alive under the Spanish name Cristóbal Colón, turned away from the sea with a sigh. There might be danger and adventure at the ends of the Earth, but at that moment he was supposed to be studying. In the pages of his books the world came alive, from the pyramids of Egypt to the island of Cipango far to the east and the lands of China where the Grand Khan was said to rule a vast land of untold riches. Beyond that were said to be lands filled with monsters and strange beasts.

Reading about faraway lands wasn't as good as visiting them for himself but thinking about his books, Christopher started to walk more quickly. He couldn't wait to find out what other places were waiting for him to discover.

1

The First Voyage

Christopher watched over the stern as the Torra della Lanterna grew smaller. With a friendly wind behind, he was sailing onto the Mediterranean. The sea air was fresh, sunlight sparkled on the water and, aside from the grumbling of sailors and the creaking ropes and timbers, all was quiet.

The ship, Christopher's new home, was one of a type called 'galleys'; narrow ships that had been used around the Mediterranean for hundreds of years. This one was about eighty feet long and fifteen feet wide, with three masts that carried square sails. Beneath the deck were benches where the crew could sit and row if the wind dropped.

The galley's sails billowed above. Below Christopher's feet, the deck rolled and the sun beat down on his face. The waving figures on the dock, his family, had already become too small to see.

Four years had passed quickly. It was now the late summer of 1465 and Christopher Columbus had just celebrated his fourteenth birthday. He had grown into a quiet, religious boy, who was often lost in a book, but he had good manners and a winning smile.

"You there! Boy!" a voice shouted. Christopher looked round to see the fierce-faced captain, Colombo, glaring at him. His father's cousin was a great, bristling, bearded bear of a man. "This isn't an afternoon pleasure trip," the captain yelled, "get to work or I'll tip you over the side."

Christopher looked around in confusion. Although he had been watching ships come and go at the port for years, he didn't have a clue what to do. He didn't have to wonder long. A grizzled sailor thrust a broom into his hands, and barked, "Get all that muck from shore off the deck."

With the breeze ruffling his hair, the boy set to work. A little later, when the captain was satisfied that everyone was busy about their jobs, he clapped Christopher on the shoulder. "Now then, boy," he said. "I promised your father I'd make a sailor of you, but don't think you'll get any favours from me just because you're some sort of nephew."

"No sir," answered Christopher, slightly scared of the captain but determined not to show it. "I'll work as hard as you like and I have studied books on navigation. I hope you'll find me useful."

"Hah, you're a book man, eh?" scoffed Colombo. "Well, you may have learned something, I suppose, but you'll soon find out that there's a lot more to taking a ship safely home than watching the stars. What do you do when the sky's all clouded over and you can't see them, eh?"

"I don't know sir," replied Christopher. "Perhaps you'd be so kind as to teach me."

Colombo looked at him closely. His years at sea had made him rough, and suspicious of polite school-room manners, but he could see the boy was nervous.

"Well, this is your first lesson," Colombo said a little more softly. "Don't go too far from shore unless you absolutely have to. So long as land's in sight you'll always have an idea where you are."

Christopher frowned. "But what about the

voyages of discovery? Surely they have to cross the oceans?"

Colombo laughed. "So you want to be one of them, do you? One of the famous navigators who goes to the edge of the world and comes back covered in fame and glory?"

Christopher Columbus nodded.

"Then your second lesson is to forget all about that," said Colombo. "There's enough danger at sea without sailing off into the strange parts where you might get eaten by cannibals or killed by monsters. On this trip we're just carrying a cargo of wine, but don't let that fool you into thinking we're safe. There might be treacherous winds that'll take us off course, or no wind at all, which can be worse. Rocks under the waves, storms that come out of nowhere, and if we see another ship it's as likely to attack us as not."

"You mean pirates?" asked Christopher.

"Pirates and the rest," laughed Colombo. "At sea everyone's a pirate if they get the chance. Sailors are always on the look out for a bit of extra money and if they see a boat they don't like the look of…"

"They attack it and steal the cargo?"

"It happens," shrugged the captain. "I've done it myself now and again." Colombo squeezed Christopher's shoulder and went on. "And it's not just money that might make a ship attack us. It's a troubled world we live in, boy. There's war everywhere and no place to escape the fighting. The best we can do is try and make a profit out of it, eh?"

Christopher thought about his parents' quiet life. They worked hard but never seemed to have much money to show for it. If he couldn't find fame and glory by sailing with Colombo, then riches would be a good start. "Yes, captain," he said with a grin. "I've always wanted to be a rich man."

The captain returned the grin. "Good lad. You stick with me and you'll get there eventually," he replied.

Although the ship wasn't big, it took Christopher all morning to clean the deck, and then there were plenty of other chores to keep him busy: ropes to coil, nets to mend and throw over the side to catch fish for the crew's supper, beer and wine to carry to the busy sailors, and all the dull, dirty jobs that no-one else wanted to do. While he worked, Christopher watched and listened to the sailors, seeing how they pulled the sails, tied a dozen different types of knot, and checked the direction of the ship against the sun. Slowly, Christopher Columbus began to learn the ways of the sea.

As the sun dipped over the horizon ahead of the ship, most of the sailors stopped work. A few men stayed on watch, steering and watching the sail, but by the light of a small oil lamp the rest sat on deck eating the hard biscuits called 'tack' and drinking wine from a barrel. Dice were brought out and a few men played each other for money while another pulled a pipe from his pocket and began to play a tune that another sang along to; a sailor's song about a girl left behind in port.

Beneath a ceiling of blazing stars, the narrow ship sailed on. It was the first of many nights that Christopher Columbus would be rocked to sleep by the waves beneath him. And, despite the warnings of the captain, all was peaceful.

2
Shipwrecked

As the months turned into years, Christopher Columbus grew into a man more at home at sea than he was on land. He became known as an excellent navigator and a clever commander and, like most sailors of his time, worked on many different ships; sometimes on trading vessels, sometimes on ships of war.

Occasionally, he still sailed with Colombo and learned to love money. In fact, Columbus's loyalty changed with whoever could pay him the most. The first time he captained a ship, he sailed to war for a French Duke. In 1474, he was alongside Colombo again, this time paid by the French King Louis XI and capturing Spanish galleys loaded with goods. The year after, he fought against the ships of Venice.

Not every voyage was so dangerous, and slowly Columbus visited many of the places he had dreamed about as a boy. He sailed to Greek trading towns and the islands of the Mediterranean Sea as well as ports along the coast of North Africa. Early in 1476 he took a cargo to Britain and went even further north, to Iceland. No one on his ship could understand the language of the Icelandic people, but if Columbus had listened to the stories of fishermen he might have heard about a land across the ocean to the west that only a few people knew existed; land that had been discovered centuries before by an explorer called Leif Ericson who had travelled there in a small longboat.

On 13 August, 1476, a few days before his twenty-fifth birthday, Columbus was again sailing with Colombo, this time in a small fleet of five ships, to attack some merchant galleys from Venice. Colombo had easily persuaded Columbus to command a ship in the attack fleet by telling him about the valuable cargo the ships would be carrying. Now, the masts of the four Venetian galleys came into view from the south, just as Colombo had said they would. With a cry of

"Oars!" Columbus pointed out the ships to the sailor manning the rudder, and felt the ship heave beneath him as sweating sailors began pulling on the oars.

All too soon, Columbus became sure that the attack was a mistake. As his galley pulled closer, he could see that the Venetian ships were much bigger than his own and well prepared for attacks. Even as they came alongside, the enemy ship began showering the small galley's deck with cannon shot and grenades. Columbus ducked while his men fastened chains to make sure the Venetian ship could not escape. Then, with a fierce shout of "Attack!" he threw himself over the side, swinging his sword.

His crew were experienced fighters and fought like tigers. Alongside them, Columbus sweated and strained, but the Venetians fought back just as fiercely. Hours later, Columbus and his crew were still nowhere close to winning. Fighting off a bearded Venetian, he spared a moment to look behind him. His own ship was on fire. Thick smoke billowed into the sky and the fire had spread to the Venetian galley. If the battle was not won soon and

19

the fire put out, both ships would burn. "Quickly, men," Columbus shouted. "We must finish this or we're all lost."

Ferociously, Columbus returned to the fight. For another hour he battled furiously on but at last the heat became too fierce. Finally, he threw his sword down, yelling "Over the side!" to his few remaining men. The two galleys, chained together, settled lower in the waves and began to sink.

Columbus thrashed around in the sea until he faced the shore. It was over six miles away. He was a strong swimmer but exhausted from fighting all day. He knew that his chances of reaching the shore alive were almost zero. There was no other choice though; all the other galleys were burning. Kicking to keep his head above water, Columbus picked at the buttons and buckles on his clothes. When only his underwear was left he started to swim. After a few strokes, his arm smacked into something; one of the galley's long wooden oars. It wasn't much, but it would help him stay afloat. Clinging to it, Columbus turned away from the sinking wreckage and drowning men and began swimming for his life.

3
Life in Lisbon

The August sun beat down on a strip of Portuguese beach. Christopher Columbus opened his eyes and pushed himself into a sitting position. Although he was bruised, burned and cut, he was still alive. Ignoring the pain, Columbus raised his eyes to the heavens and clasped his hands together in prayer.

"O Lord God," he sobbed. "I am saved. Why have you done this? Do you have a purpose for me? Some great task I must achieve?"

With tears streaming down his sunburned face, Columbus dragged himself further up the shore.

It took weeks for his wounds to heal and more than a month for his strength to return. As he recovered, Columbus made his way north through sleepy towns and fishing villages until he reached the Portuguese capital city of Lisbon. There he threw himself into the welcoming arms of his younger brother, who had recently moved to the city to become a map maker.

"Christopher," said Bartholomew Columbus as the two men ate a roasted chicken in Bartholomew's room that evening, "with all these years you've spent at sea, it is a wonder that you're not dead in some battle or drowned yet. Why not stay with me for a while? You would be safe on shore and there is enough work for both of us. New maps are always needed. I know you learned to draw back in Genoa."

"The sea is my life," replied Christopher, "and I am sure that God saved me for a reason."

"What reason?"

"I don't know," Christopher admitted.

"Then stay here until you know what God wishes you to do," said Bartholomew. "There's a chapel along the road. You will be able to pray for his help there."

Christopher was silent for a few moments, then he nodded. Although he would still go to sea now and again, for the next sixteen years his life and work would be mostly on land.

Lisbon, like Genoa, was one of Europe's great sea ports and a city known for learning and adventure. Under King Henry the Navigator, Portugal had been at the centre of the voyages of discovery. Though King Henry was now dead, Columbus felt at home in the exciting, bustling city.

While he settled into his new life, Columbus did not forget his belief that God had a plan for him. He often prayed at the small chapel of All Saints close to Bartholomew's cramped rooms. Before long, he found himself glancing at a woman who also prayed there, her beautiful head bowed as she knelt before the altar surrounded by billowing skirts and with her long, dark hair drawn into a knot at the back of her neck. Doña Filipa de Perestrello was a noblewoman, the daughter of one of Lisbon's most famous navigators. Noticing that the handsome young man often looked towards her, Filipa began to give him shy smiles in return and, after a while, Columbus plucked up the courage to talk to her. Soon, they fell in love and, in 1479, they were married.

After the wedding, Columbus moved into

his wife's family home. At dinner that night, he charmed Filipa's mother with his beautiful manners and quiet smile. As the plates were taken away, she leaned toward him and said, "You remind me of my husband."

"Thank you, my lady," Columbus replied, bowing his head. "Your husband was a great man."

"You know," the old lady continued, "I still have all of his maps and diaries in a chest upstairs. Would you like to see them?"

To be allowed to look at the charts of a great navigator would be a dream come true. With an excited grin, Columbus replied, "Oh yes, my lady. Yes indeed. It would be almost as great an honour as marrying his daughter."

Soon after, the newly married couple set out for the island of Porto Santo where Filipa had inherited a house. It was an exciting time. Filipa was expecting their first child and her sister lived on the island with her husband, the navigator Pedro Correo. Porto Santo was a busy port and to Columbus it was like being a boy again, living so close to a harbour where everyone was talking about voyages of discovery. With his own dreams of adventure reawakened by the dockside talk and Filipa's father's diaries, Columbus found himself longing for adventure, and he often sat up late with Correo, planning voyages they would like to make. Perhaps, Columbus thought, he had at last found out God's plan for him. Perhaps he was supposed to make a great voyage of discovery.

He began to spend all his evenings at his desk, surrounded by maps and papers. One evening as Columbus sat hunched over his charts and books Filipa came and laid a hand on his shoulder.

"Look at this, my love," said Columbus, pointing to the map spread out on the table and pulling the flickering candle closer so that his wife could see better. "Here is Portugal, on the very western edge of Europe. And to the east are Spain, France, Italy, Greece, and then the Empire of the Ottomans to the far distant lands of Asia: Persia, India and beyond. No-one knows how far those lands stretch."

His wife nodded gently.

"All trade with the east is by land." Columbus traced the route with a finger. "It is a long and dangerous road across many countries and thousands of miles, over treacherous mountains and through great deserts. There are bandits along every mile. Along this road spices and silks and all the treasures of the East must be carried."

His wife sighed. "Everyone knows this, Christopher," she said. "It is why some hope it is possible to reach Asia by sailing around Africa, though no-one dares to make the journey."

"Yes," replied her husband. "Everyone talks of going around Africa, because whoever did sail to Asia would open a sea route to the riches of the East. No goods would ever need to travel by land again."

Columbus's fingers drummed on the map. "But what if sailing around Africa was not the right way?" he whispered. "What if you might reach Asia by sailing in the opposite direction?"

A frown crossed Filipa's face. "I don't understand," she said.

"Look again," Columbus said, pointing at the map once more. "We know that the Earth is round; a great globe."

"Of course," replied his wife. "Only fools still believe the world is flat. Any sailor can tell you that's not true."

"Well then," continued Columbus in greater excitement. "If the lands of Asia stretch far to the east it should be possible to reach the coasts that lie furthest away from us by sailing directly to the west."

He made an unfinished circle on a piece of paper and ran his finger round it. "See, here is Portugal, and stretching almost all the way around the rest of the world is land." He pointed to the small part of the circle his pen had not finished. "And this is the Atlantic Ocean. By crossing it, a ship would arrive here," he jabbed a finger, "at the far eastern coast of Asia."

"Sail across the Atlantic?" Filipa whispered in amazement. "But no-one would try and sail across the great ocean. They say that it goes on forever. There are storms that throw up waves the size of mountains, and who knows what monsters... It is madness to even think about making such a voyage."

Columbus leaned back in his chair. "Yes," he said. "It would take great courage. But if the world is round then the Atlantic cannot go on forever. That would be impossible."

At that moment the look of amazement on Filipa's face was replaced by one of fierce pain. She cried out and her hand clutched at her swollen stomach. "Christopher," she gasped. "I think it is time."

A few hours later Christopher Columbus held a baby boy, who he named Diego. For the moment, his plan to reach the far eastern lands of Asia was forgotten. It was a plan no-one had ever thought of before, and Columbus was almost right. He had made two mistakes, however. Firstly, the globe was a lot bigger than he imagined and the distance between the west of Europe and the east of Asia was enormous. His second mistake was that he did not guess that other lands might exist. In fact, across the Atlantic, between Europe and Asia, lay the great continents of North and South America.

4
Stormy Weather

Slowly, the idea that he might land in Asia by sailing across the Atlantic filled Christopher Columbus's every waking hour. In 1482, Filipa died of a sickness. Grief-stricken, Columbus sailed back to Lisbon with his young son and lost himself in his books and charts. As the months passed, he became more and more certain that God had spared his life from the shipwreck so that he could discover the way to Asia. He began writing letters explaining his idea to scientists and great thinkers around Europe. A few of them sent him their own maps and charts in return.

The great Atlantic voyage became Columbus's passion and he neglected his business. He grew poorer, and often there was little for him and Diego to eat. Sorrow and hardship began to turn

Columbus's sandy hair to grey. Nevertheless, he never stopped thinking of his plans. To make his voyage he would need a rich supporter to pay for the ships, stocked with food, as well as the men he needed. Columbus's first thought was of the young king John II of Portugal. Like his great uncle, Henry the Navigator, John II was known for his love of adventure and discovery. Columbus wrote to him asking to be allowed to present his plan and, in 1484, his requests were successful.

After listening to Columbus, the Portuguese king betrayed him. Thinking that Columbus's plans were too expensive, the king ordered a single ship to sail across the Atlantic to find out if Columbus was right and a route to Asia could be found. The voyage lasted only a handful of days. Faced with storms and the endless waves of the great ocean, the captain and crew soon returned to Lisbon, telling King John that there was nothing but certain death to be found on the Atlantic.

The treacherous voyage could not remain secret long and word soon reached Columbus. Furious, he packed his precious books and charts and left Portugal the same day.

In 1485, he visited first his home city of Genoa, and then Venice. The rulers of both cities refused to pay for his voyage. Disheartened and alone, Columbus travelled to Spain where the country's two rulers, King Ferdinand and Queen Isabella, were fighting against the Moorish people of Northern Africa who had ruled parts of the country for over 600 years. The two rulers were loaded down with the cares of war and it was impossible for Columbus to see them, but his plans brought him to the attention of the Duke of Medina Celi, a rich and powerful man who kept his own small fleet of ships. The Duke was impressed and almost offered Columbus his own ships to use for the voyage. However, he realized that if Columbus was successful, the king and queen would be displeased if the riches that might be found in Asia fell into his hands and not theirs. Instead, he wrote to Queen Isabella telling her about Columbus's scheme.

Within weeks, a letter came from the Queen herself. Columbus, it said, was to present himself at court in the Spanish city of Cordova.

In Cordova, Columbus found a city that shook to the marching feet of soldiers and glinted with the armour of steel-clad knights on horseback. At the centre of all the activity were Isabella and Ferdinand. Together, the King and Queen organized their armies, pored over maps and battle plans, and involved themselves in every detail of the war. Often, they followed their men into battle, returning only to celebrate a victory before riding off again. Every second of Ferdinand and Isabella's time was precious and, as Columbus soon found out, none could be spared for an unknown sailor.

Columbus waited to see the King and Queen for month after month. Sometimes he was summoned to speak to court officials and the royal advisors. A few were interested in his plans but none had the power to give him the money and ships he needed. Most of the time, Columbus had little to do. He was given comfortable rooms though and, as 1485 passed into 1486, he fell in love again. Like Filipa, Beatrix Enriquez was a woman of noble birth whose family had fallen on hard times and, like Filipa, she soon became pregnant. Columbus's second son, Fernando, was born in 1487 and would one day write his father's story for the world to read.

Late in 1486, Columbus was finally given a

chance to present his plan to King Ferdinand. Showing his maps and papers, Columbus explained to the cold-faced King how he planned to discover the eastern coasts of Asia by sailing west across the Atlantic. Ferdinand was a cautious man who disliked spending money. He was interested in the plan but ordered that a meeting of educated men should come together in the Spanish city of Salamanca to discuss it. Their report would decide the matter.

Again, Columbus was forced to travel and to present his ideas to another audience. Most of them were men of the church and only knew about the old writings of dead saints. They understood little of geography and many even believed that the Earth was flat. On the very first day of the meetings, one old priest got to his feet. "Is there anyone so foolish," he sneered, "as to believe that on the other side of the world there are men who walk upside down and where it rains upwards?"

Columbus squeezed his eyes shut to stop himself from crying. It would be impossible, he thought, to make men like this understand his plan. Even so, he had no choice. Standing, Columbus began to talk in his good-mannered and dignified way. Years of study and careful thought gave his words weight, and day after day he patiently showed the dusty old men his maps and explained his ideas. Slowly, he won a handful of supporters.

At the end of the meetings, Columbus left the men to argue among themselves and returned to Beatrix in Cordova. Months passed and no report arrived from Salamanca. The war still raged and Columbus was ignored by the King and Queen. Desperate, he began writing to the rulers of other countries. A letter was sent to the King of France and Columbus's brother Bartholomew agreed to travel to England to plead with King Henry VII. Fearing that he would never make his voyage, Columbus even wrote to John II of Portugal again.

By 1491 Columbus had still heard nothing. Tired and angry, he asked the royal advisors to request that the King and Queen make a decision. Instead, Isabella and Ferdinand sent to Salamanca for the report that had still not come. When it finally arrived, Columbus was horrified to find that the old men had decided that a voyage across the Atlantic was impossible.

Only one hope remained: Queen Isabella thought Columbus's plan was a good idea, though she and Ferdinand still refused to say whether they would pay for it. This time, Columbus was told that he must wait until the war was over for an answer.

After six years of waiting, Columbus had reached the end of his patience. Dressed in poor clothes and almost penniless he left the Spanish court and began walking towards the coast. He planned to take a ship to France and try his luck there.

A few days later, sweating beneath the hot sun, Columbus stopped at a lonely, yellow-stoned monastery to beg some water and a little bread from the monks. While he drank, the head of the monastery, Prior Juan Perez de Marchena, happened to pass by and stopped to find out who the stranger was. Columbus was quick to tell him of his plans and his disappointments at court. As the story poured out, the prior's eyes widened in amazement. All day and into the night, he listened to Columbus, and as he listened he became sure that the Spanish King and Queen had made a terrible mistake in allowing Columbus to leave.

As soon as he woke the following morning, the

prior rushed to his desk where he wrote a letter to the Queen, whom he had known for many years, telling her of his certainty that the Columbus was right. It would, he wrote, be a disaster for Spain if another country were first to discover Asia by Columbus's route.

When Isabella received the prior's letter she was finally stung into action. Columbus was sent money and told to return to court immediately. The queen wrote that this time he could be certain of having her full attention.

With his hope reawakened, Columbus rode back along the dusty road towards the city of Grenada where the Spanish army had defeated the Moors. He could not have returned at a better time. Finally, the war was over and the city was in celebration.

Free from the troubles of war, Queen Isabella kept her word. As soon as the victory ceremonies were finished, the tired but joyful Queen summoned Columbus to her rooms. Unlike her cool husband, the queen was a generous ruler with a kind nature and Columbus's good manners charmed her. She was also clever, and could see the sense in Columbus's plan. At last, he had a royal supporter with the power to make his voyage a reality.

Only one more obstacle stood in his way: money. Since childhood Columbus had dreamed of fame and riches and now he had his chance to make his dreams come true. He asked for a tenth of all the riches he found, to be made the governor of any new lands he discovered and also to be made an Admiral, an important job that would immediately make him a nobleman. His last request was that his older son, Diego, should be given a place at court as a page boy, so that he might grow up among nobles and royalty and become a gentleman.

Queen Isabella was amazed by his demands. How could an unknown sailor ask for so much, no matter what he might discover? The cost of the voyage, too, was more than she could afford. Within a few days, Columbus was told that the Queen supported his plan, but she could not afford to pay for it.

Furious that his time had been wasted, Columbus left the palace and rode away from Grenada.

Word of his departure spread quickly around the court until it reached the ears of Luis de Sant Angel, one of the few men who had been a supporter of Columbus at the meetings in Salamanca. As soon as he heard, de Sant Angel rushed to the queen.

"Your majesty," he blurted out as he bowed before Queen Isabella. "Columbus has left. It is a disaster for Spain."

The Queen shook her head. "It is to be expected," she said sadly. "The price was high and Spain's money has been spent on war."

Falling to his knees, de Sant Angel begged Isabella to think again. "But my Queen," he panted, "is the price really so high when we think of what Columbus might find? It is a risk, yes. His ships might never return. But if he is successful think of the wealth he might bring back. Think how Spain's power might spread to distant corners of the world. And then think how Columbus might give all this to another country; that the glory and riches might go to France or Portugal or even England. I beg your majesty not to let Columbus leave."

Isabella stared at him. For a moment she sat silent, then the queen stood and spoke commandingly.

"Send horses after Columbus," she ordered. "Tell him that he shall have his ships whatever the price. Tell him he will have them even if I have to sell my own jewels."

5
1492

Christopher Columbus stood on the deck of the *Santa Maria*, holding onto a rope and watching the distant horizon. Now forty-two years old, he felt the thrill of adventure of a young boy on his first voyage. Behind him was the small Spanish port of Palos at the head of the River Saltes. Ahead was the wide Atlantic Ocean, glittering beneath the early morning sun.

Not far away, two other ships kept pace with the *Santa Maria* – the *Nina* and the *Pinta*, ships of a type called 'caravels'. Each had three masts that carried square and triangular sails that could be moved to catch the wind. At the front and back – or 'fore' and 'aft' as the sailors said – they had high decks and in between they were open to the sun and rain. Columbus's ship, the *Santa Maria*, was called a 'nao'. Bigger than the *Pinta* and *Nina*, she was bulky and slow and Columbus was not at all sure that she was the right type for a voyage of discovery, though he was grateful to have any ships at all.

For a few moments he allowed himself a grin, then he set his face in the stern expression of an admiral and turned back to his crew.

Every man on board was terrified. Only the captains of the other two ships – Martin Alonzo Pinzon on the *Pinta* and his brother Vincente Yañez Pinzon on the *Nina* – had joined the voyage willingly; the rest of the sailors had come on board on the King and Queen's orders and under threat of punishment. They were certain that the three ships sailed to their doom and many of the sailors had done everything they could to delay the voyage or escape sailing. The scenes had been terrible as the three ships left Palos at dawn. Men, women, and children had clung to each other sobbing as they said farewell to their husbands, fathers and brothers who sailed with Columbus.

Columbus walked the deck, giving orders and directions, making sure that every man on board had enough work to take his mind off the dangers ahead. That night, he began the diary he would keep throughout the voyage. He was too exhausted to write much, but set down how the voyage had begun.

Friday, 3 August.

We departed Friday 3rd day of August 1492 from Saltes at the eighth hour. We proceeded with strong sea winds until the setting of the sun toward the south sixty miles which are fifteen leagues; afterwards to the southwest and south by west, which was the course to the Canaries.

Columbus had decided that the Canary Islands, which were 700 miles from the coast of Spain in the Atlantic Ocean, would make a good stopping point. There, he could take on fresh water and allow the crew some time on land before making the longer journey across the Atlantic. Halfway through August, as the three ships came close to the islands, the frightened men on board the *Pinta* tried to delay the voyage. They broke the ship's rudder, leaving the *Pinta* at the mercy of the winds. For three weeks, Columbus was forced to keep the ships in harbour while the *Pinta* was repaired until, on 6 September, he gave the order to set sail, and the *Santa Maria* led the *Pinta* and *Nina* out into the Atlantic. The voyage into the unknown had now truly begun. It was time to find out if Columbus was right, if the lands of Asia lay across the Atlantic Ocean.

For three days the ships moved slowly across calm water. Late on 9 September, however, a stiff breeze picked up and the sails began to crack and billow. Columbus saw that the wind was coming from the east and would blow the ships in exactly the right direction. "West! Due west!" he shouted to the pilot. "And signal the *Nina* and *Pinta* to make the same course."

The ships swept across the Atlantic for the next ten days, crossing 1,500 miles of empty ocean at a good speed. Gradually, the sailors became less fearful. The breeze and calm seas were perfect for sailing and, for once, they did not have to worry about pirates. Columbus was careful to keep from his men exactly how far they had travelled, letting them believe that they were closer to home than they really were.

The following week was more difficult. The winds changed, slowing the ships' progress and, again, the sailors began to mutter about turning back. Columbus often walked the deck, reminding each man of the treasure they were sure to find. On one occasion, he pointed to a bird crossing the sky above the *Santa Maria*'s mast. "Look there," he called. "It's a tern. Those birds never fly far from land. We are getting closer now."

Days passed and still no land appeared, though the sailors began to see strange things. For a while they sailed through thick seaweed in the calm part of the Atlantic that is now called the Sargasso Sea.

Again, Columbus told them this was a sure sign that land was not far ahead. A few days later, a whale was spotted. The sailors rushed to the sides and watched in awe as the great creature spouted water far into the air and cracked the surface with its massive tail.

Another week passed. By now the Canary Islands were 2,000 miles behind and the grumbles of the sailors were growing into demands that Columbus turn the ships around. On 10 October, more than a month after his men had last seen land, Columbus wrote in his diary, "Here the people could stand it no longer, and complained of the long voyage." As before, the admiral went among his crew, telling them they would soon find riches. The wind blew again from the east and the three ships scudded onwards into the unknown, across the seemingly never-ending ocean.

The next day, just as Columbus was beginning to think that his sailors might turn against him, there came a certain sign that land was close. A length of wood was pulled from the water. On it were carvings made by a human hand. Knowing this meant that there were people somewhere not far ahead, the men were filled with new hope. Beneath clear blue skies and warmed by a friendly sun, some jumped from the deck and swam around the ships, pointing with delight at the dolphins that played around them.

To cheer his men even more, Columbus reminded the crews of all three ships that the King and Queen had promised a reward to the first man who sighted land. Many times the air rang with the shouts of excited sailors imagining that they saw land. And though each sighting turned out to be false, still the sailors watched the horizon eagerly.

At eleven o'clock on the night of 11 October, Columbus was walking the deck of the *Santa Maria*, checking that all was well. Stopping for a moment to look out into the bright, moonlit night, he saw a small light moving close to the horizon, like a lamp in the distance. Unable to believe his eyes, he called two men over. Both saw the same thing. Trembling with excitement, Columbus ordered that a message should be sent to the *Nina* and *Pinta*, warning them to keep a close watch ahead and then turned back to look again. The light had disappeared.

LIVESinACTION

Four hours later, the lookout high in the *Pinta's* rigging shouted "Land! Land!" Every sailor on the three ships instantly woke and rushed to see. Before them, under the light of a full moon, was the unmistakable dark bulk of an island. After more than ten years of study and argument, waiting and disappointment, Christopher Columbus at last knew that he had been right. There was land across the Atlantic. With tears in his eyes, he sank to his knees and gave thanks to God for bringing the ships safely across the ocean. Ahead, he believed, lay the lands of Asia.

He was wrong, though. The three ships had discovered an island that lay off the south-eastern coast of what would, in time, become known as Florida. Columbus had found America.

6

Columbus in Paradise

Columbus leaned over the ship's rail as the sun rose the next morning, gazing at the island. Set in clear, green sea and surrounded by white beaches, it looked like paradise. Countless trees rose from low hills and colourful flowers blossomed among thick bushes. Parrots flitted among the branches and exotic smells wafted out to sea. On the shore was a crowd of people, staring the three ships in astonishment. All of them had long, black hair and all of them were naked. On the warm island clothes were not needed. Because of this, Columbus thought they must be savages though, in fact, the people had a simple, peaceful way of life that was perfectly suited to their island home.

"To where have you brought me, God?" Columbus whispered. "Is this China or Cipango?

Or India? Are these people Indians?"

"May I speak to you, Lord Admiral?" asked a sailor behind Columbus, interrupting his thoughts.

Columbus looked round, surprised to see the sailor, who had been one of the most troublesome during the voyage. The man bowed. "I am deeply sorry that I did not trust you, Lord Admiral," he said. "You were right, and we were wrong to say that we would never find land across the ocean. I give you my word that you will never hear me complain again and the same goes for every man aboard."

"I thank you, and all this brave crew," Columbus replied loudly so that every man could hear him. As they cheered, he smiled and said, "Now, let us go ashore and see what there is to discover. Lower the longboats!"

A short while later, the boat that carried Columbus ashore crunched on sand. Dressed in his finest clothes, the Admiral stepped through the surf and onto the shore. Dropping to his knees, he thanked God again, kissed the ground, then stood and waved at the sailors to come ashore.

As the island people watched in amazement,

Columbus displayed the flags of the King and Queen of Spain. They saw him plant a banner in the sand and speak words in a language they had never heard. "In the name of their majesties, Isabella and Ferdinand," Columbus said, "I claim this land as a possession of Spain and name it San Salvador."

With these words the island, where the ancestors of the watching folk had lived for a thousand years or more, became the property of a country 3,000 miles across the sea. None of the island's people understood what had happened that day, but soon they would know all too well what it meant to be ruled by the Spanish. For the moment though, they could contain their curiosity no longer. Laughing and shouting, the islanders rushed towards Columbus and his men, reaching out to touch their soft clothes and pale skin. Columbus made a sign and a sailor brought forward a small chest as if it contained great riches. It was filled with glass beads, bells, and mirrors: cheap, colourful things that Columbus had brought along to impress people who might not have seen such trinkets before.

The islanders took them from Columbus's hands with shouts of joy. They believed that the strange visitors had come from the sky with gifts of friendship.

All that day, the men of the *Santa Maria*, *Nina*, and *Pinta* explored the island. The islanders did not seem bothered by the strangers going into their neat, palm-thatched huts and looking through their few belongings, and brought the sailors fish and fruit to eat. The sailors wandered among great groves of trees, exclaiming at the bright birds above, or else they splashed in the shallow sea, amazed at the dazzling colours of coral and the fish that darted about.

There was one colour that Columbus particularly wanted to see, though: one that would convince Ferdinand and Isabella that his voyage had been worthwhile and which would make him rich. That colour was gold and, soon, Columbus saw it. In the late afternoon, the Admiral glimpsed the unmistakable flash of the precious metal in a ring that one of the island people wore through his nose. Catching at the man's arm, Columbus pointed at it and offered the man some beads, which he happily swapped for his jewellery.

"Where can I find more of this?" Columbus asked, pointing at the gold and then throwing out his arm, hoping the islander would understand.

The young man pointed across the sea to the south west. Columbus gestured to the gold again and then in the same direction as the young islander. The man grinned with delight and held out his arms and staggered along the beach as if weighed down by a heavy load.

Columbus turned to Martin Pinzon next to him and whispered, "Is he telling us that there is more gold in that direction? Enough that it would be difficult to carry?"

"It seems likely," answered Pinzon. "We should go and find out as soon as possible."

Columbus nodded. Later that day, he found other islanders who wore small amounts of gold. Each of them gave him their precious jewellery freely and always pointed in the same direction when Columbus asked them in signs and gestures where he could find more.

Eager to find more treasure, Columbus sailed from San Salvador the next morning. He took with him all the gold he had been able to find and seven of the islanders, whom the Spanish sailors were now calling "Indians" because they believed they were somewhere close to India. The Admiral hoped that his new passengers would learn Spanish and act as interpreters, and he also knew that they would cause a great stir at the Spanish court. There was another, darker reason for taking them, too. In Columbus's time it was common for Europeans to capture people like the islanders, tear them from their homes and families, and sell them as slaves. The handsome, healthy folk he had found on San Salvador would fetch a good price in the slave markets of Spain.

While Indians swam around the *Nina*, *Pinta* and *Santa Maria*, or paddled around the ships in their long canoes, Columbus gave his orders to the pilot. The ships turned to the south west. Ahead, Columbus was sure, lay the Asian cities he had read about so many times, where it was said that the houses had roof tiles of solid gold.

Over the following days, the explorers discovered many new islands. On every one, the people were as simple and kind as the Indians of San Salvador.

They brought food to Columbus and his crew and treated the sailors as gods who had appeared from the sky. On each island though, Columbus found only a few scraps of gold and the people always pointed onwards to the south west when Columbus asked where more could be found. Now, however, they gave a name to the place that was rich in gold, calling it 'Cuba' in their own language. From their signs, Columbus understood this to be a great, rich land, much larger than any of the islands. At last, he thought, he was getting closer to the mainland of whatever Asian country he had arrived at.

On 24 October, 1492, Columbus sailed south from an island he had named Isabella in the Queen's honour. He found Cuba four days later, and was soon convinced that it was the land he had been looking for. From the deck of the *Santa Maria* he could see tall mountains far inland and the coast stretched away as far as the eye could see. It was obvious that this was no small island like those he had already visited.

7

The Golden Isle

Using signs, the Indians that Columbus had brought on board the *Santa Maria* said that three days' journey inland from the coast of Cuba was a place they called 'Cubanacan'. In their language 'Cuba' was the name of the island and 'nacan' meant 'inland'. By saying 'Cuba nacan' they were trying to tell Columbus about a village away from the shore of Cuba, but Columbus misunderstood them and thought Cubanacan must be the name of a great golden city.

He sent two men to Cubanacan, loaded with gifts and letters for the great prince who might live there, and settled down to wait for their return. The rest of the sailors were ordered to clean and repair the ships or to search the forests and meadows for plants and spices that might be valuable. So far from Europe, and from Asia, there was nothing they recognised but during their searches, the Spanish sailors became the first to see something that would be on every European table in the years to come: the potato.

On 6 November, the two men and their guides returned. As soon as he saw their long faces, Columbus's heart sank.

"It was a wasted journey, Lord Admiral," one of the weary men began. "It is true that there is a village three days' travel inland but it has no gold and is hardly bigger than any we have seen so far. It is certainly not the capital of a great prince."

Columbus nodded, trying to hide his disappointment, and listened as the men described the lands they had seen on their journey, the chieftain they had met, and the birds and animals to be found further inland. Little of it interested him; it was gold he cared for. Gold would make the difference between returning to Spain with stories of discovering poor islands far across the ocean, and returning to wealth and fame. No matter how beautiful the islands were, the King and Queen would not be happy unless these lands could provide Spain with riches.

He began to despair of ever finding the fabulous cities of Asia, but he knew that there must be gold close by. The Indians had given him small scraps and all of them believed that there was an island just over the horizon where lumps of the precious metal could be picked up like seashells on the beach.

Again Columbus set sail, taking more men and women from their homes. Nearby was gold, he was certain of it. The new Indians pointed to the east and spoke the words "Bohio" and "Babeque" when he showed them his small golden treasures. Columbus was sure that these must be the names of the islands where he could find what he was looking for. For a few days the three ships swept along the coast of Cuba and then the Admiral gave the order to change direction and the *Santa Maria* led the *Nina* and *Pinta* eastwards in search of Babeque and Bohio.

On 20 November, the sea became rough for the first time since the ships had arrived among the islands. The decks rolled beneath the sailors' feet, rain whipped at their faces, and the wind blew stronger. It was not as great a storm as some that Columbus had seen in his years at sea but gradually the *Pinta* was blown further and further away. Columbus ordered signals to be raised telling Martin Pinzon, the *Pinta's* captain, to turn back. It made no difference. As he watched, the *Pinta* vanished over the horizon. All that night, the *Nina* and *Santa Maria* burned lights to guide their lost sister ship back to them, but in the morning the sea was empty. The *Pinta* had gone.

Columbus was beside himself with worry. Not from the fear that the *Pinta* might have been wrecked, but because she was a faster ship than either the *Nina* or *Santa Maria*. As the two remaining ships turned around in the heaving seas and headed back to the safety of Cuba, Columbus wondered gloomily if Pinzon had decided to sail back towards Spain. If the *Pinta* arrived home first, Columbus knew he would find his discovery had been stolen. Pinzon would always be remembered as the captain who had brought home the news of the islands across the Atlantic.

For two weeks the two ships sailed around Cuba. Then, on 5 December, one of the Indians pointed to a mountainous island on the far horizon and shouted "Babeque! Babeque!"

"Turn about! To the east!" ordered Columbus immediately. "Sail to that island."

Babeque was as lovely as any island Columbus had seen so far, with sweeping meadows and lofty mountains. But, again, there was not a sign of gold. For several days, Columbus explored until he was forced to admit that the Indians had been wrong again. Frustrated, he ordered the two ships out to sea.

Day after day, the *Santa Maria* and *Nina* sailed from island to island. The admiral gave new Spanish names to all of them but never found more than a trace of gold. A few days before Christmas, the two ships anchored off an island that Columbus named 'Hispaniola', which is now two countries known as Haiti and the Dominican Republic. As often happened, the native people swam and paddled out in their canoes to see the strange visitors and were allowed aboard by the sailors.

A few days later, Columbus welcomed a new group of Indians and through signs and gestures he was told that they brought gifts from a chieftain called Guacanagari whose village was further down the coast. Politely, Columbus held out his hands and thanked an old Indian as he was handed a belt, beautifully made from bone, shells, and coral. Then his eyes widened. The Indian was holding out another gift: a large mask, its eyes, nose, and tongue gleaming with an unmistakable colour. At last Columbus had found the gold he was searching for.

Ordering that the Indians should be given gifts of glass beads in return, Columbus eagerly questioned the old man and found out that there was more gold in Guacanagari's village. The Admiral waved one of his men over.

"When this Indian leaves," he said, "take a few others and go back to his village with him. Find out if there is any truth in what he says."

Taking a chest full of cheap gifts, the men departed. For a few days Columbus was left in a state of excitement as he waited for their return. Meanwhile, Indians from other parts of Hispaniola arrived, and each told him that the island was rich in gold. When his men arrived back at the ship with more golden gifts, Columbus could wait no longer.

LIVESinACTION

On the morning of Christmas Eve, the *Santa Maria* and *Nina* set sail for Guacanagari's village.

It was a short voyage but not one that could be made in one day. As the stars came out that night, Columbus realised how tired he was. Usually he liked to stay on deck while the ships were under sail, watching for danger, but it was a calm night and he decided that for once he would sleep. Telling the pilot that he had command of the *Santa Maria*, Columbus went to his cabin.

As soon as Columbus had gone, the pilot turned to one of the ship's boys.

"Here, take this," he said, pointing at the ship's wheel. "The Admiral's not the only man who needs some rest."

"But it's against orders," said the boy unhappily. "The Admiral said…"

"Never mind what he said," hissed the pilot. "You take the wheel while I get some sleep. And if you ever tell, I'll have your skin."

Nervously, the boy obeyed. Taking the great wheel with shaking hands he steered the *Santa Maria* onward through calm water.

As the night wore on, the young lad relaxed.

"Why, this is easy," he muttered to himself. "Old Columbus should let me take the wheel all the time."

Just then, he felt a gentle crunch beneath his feet and heard the sound of waves breaking on the shore close by. In the darkness, his face went pale and he began to tremble again. He swung the wheel from side to side, but the *Santa Maria* was no longer moving.

"Run aground!" shouted the boy with fear in his voice.

The next morning, Columbus watched in fury from the *Nina* as waves pushed the *Santa Maria* further onto the coral reef she had hit the night before. All the sailors' efforts to pull her off had failed. The *Santa Maria* was taking in water through several holes in her side and it was only a matter of time before she broke up completely. Nothing could be done except strip the ship of everything valuable before she sank.

The admiral cursed under his breath. One small caravel is all I have left now, he thought to himself bitterly. The tiny *Nina* was the only vessel that could get him and all his men back to Spain, and if she, too, was lost then no-one would ever know of his discoveries.

At least the *Santa Maria* had come within a few miles of Guacanagari's village before disaster struck. Messages had been sent to the chieftain and now canoes began to appear in the distance. Columbus's heavy heart lightened a little as he watched the friendly natives pour onboard the sinking ship and help the struggling sailors to load her food and provisions into longboats and canoes.

As if to make up for the loss of the *Santa Maria*, Guacanagari arrived on board the *Nina* with more gold the next morning, 26 December. Columbus took a liking to the cheerful Indian chieftain, who was keen to help the visitors in any way he could. Using signs, Guacanagari invited Columbus to stay in his village. Columbus agreed and followed with a small company of men as Guacanagari led the way along paths lined with magnificent blossoms to a large, neat village that had been freshly swept.

Beneath the branches of great trees, heavy with fruit, Columbus found gold. As soon as they arrived at the village Guacanagari hung plates of it around the admiral's neck and offered him a crown made from the precious metal. Other villagers brought nuggets that they were happy to give away for nothing, though Columbus always made sure that they took away a gift in return. At last Columbus knew he could return to Spain with news that would please the King and Queen. Here was gold in plenty.

While Columbus stared at the growing pile of metal in front of him, a plan began to form in his mind. It would be difficult to take all his men home on the little *Nina*, but if he left some of them here, they could search for more gold until he returned. By the time that Columbus had been to Spain and back there might be a great treasure trove waiting for him. Maybe his men might even find the mines where the gold came from.

Guacanagari seemed delighted with Columbus's plan. Together, the Admiral and the Indian chieftain searched out a good spot where a small fortress could be built from wood taken from the wreck of the *Santa Maria*. The islanders helped the Spanish to build it and with so many men the work was quickly done. At the same time, Guacanagari sent more men to find as much gold as they could for Columbus's stores.

After a few days, the fortress was built. Columbus picked out men from the many volunteers who wanted to stay on the island, and named the fortress La Navidad. Now that the *Nina* was loaded with gold, Columbus was keen to return to Spain. Giving the men who were staying at La Navidad strict orders to behave kindly towards the Indians, Columbus said farewell to Guacanagari and boarded his last ship for the 3,000 mile journey back across the ocean. The date was 4 January 1493.

Two days later, a lookout cried out from the mast above Columbus's head. On the horizon were the sails of the lost *Pinta*.

8

Return to Glory

In Columbus's cabin that evening, Martin Pinzon told the Admiral that the *Pinta* had been blown off course during the storm and that he had been sailing around the islands looking for Columbus ever since. Although Columbus thought that it was more likely that Pinzon had gone to look for gold on his own, he was relieved that he had not sailed back to Spain after all and welcomed the *Pinta*'s captain joyfully. Together again, the two caravels began the long voyage back to Spain.

At first the wind was against them, making progress slow but halfway across the Atlantic the breeze changed and the ships sailed on quickly until 12 February. Now, however, the weather grew much colder and the sky ahead was dark. Frowning, Columbus watched the heavy, black clouds roll towards him.

"A bad storm coming, Admiral," said a bearded sailor next to him.

"With God's help it will pass us by," replied Columbus with more hope than he felt.

By that evening the most ferocious gale that Columbus had ever seen was all around them. The men aboard the caravels lost count of the hours, and then the days, as they were lashed by rain and hailstones. Towering seas threatened to capsize the small, open-decked caravels at any moment and huge, iron-grey waves crashed over them until every man was soaked and shivering with cold and fear. Columbus shouted orders at his terrified men as the *Nina* was tossed this way and that but there was little that any of them could do except pray. The *Pinta* was soon lost again and, in desperation, Columbus wrote a letter to Isabella and Ferdinand telling them of his discoveries, then tossed it over the side in a barrel. If the ship sank, as seemed certain, his great news might still be found.

Through the storm the small ship bucked and lurched with its terrified crew. Then, when all hope had been lost, land was sighted. Columbus's men wept for joy as the *Nina* made her way to the harbour of St Mary's on an Atlantic island that belonged to Portugal.

Their troubles were not at an end though. As the crew made their way to church to thank God, the island's governor took them prisoner. Columbus was forced to threaten war on Portugal in the King and Queen's name before they were released.

When his crew returned, Columbus took the *Nina* out into the stormy sea as quickly as possible. On 2 March, the howling wind tore her sails away. For two days the small caravel was tossed on mountainous waves before land was sighted again.

The people of the small Portuguese port of Rastello watched, amazed, as the *Nina* was blown towards them through a storm that no ship should have been able to survive. A great cheer went up from his crew as the ship finally anchored in a safe harbour but still Columbus faced danger. King John II soon found out that the Admiral was sheltering in one of his ports and that he had sailed across the Atlantic and back. Jealous that Columbus's discoveries had been made for Spain and not Portugal, King John demanded to see

Columbus and kept him away from his ship for almost two weeks, during which the Admiral was in constant fear that the traitorous king was be plotting to have him imprisoned, or worse.

Finally, however, the *Nina* was allowed to leave and, on 15 March 1493, after a voyage of more than seven months, she found her way back to the Spanish harbour of Palos. On shore, the townsfolk could hardly believe their eyes. They had never expected to see the ship or the men aboard again. As news of Columbus's safe return and his discoveries spread, rejoicing and celebration swept through the port.

When the *Nina* was safely tied up, Columbus hastily began making his preparations to travel north to the King and Queen in Barcelona. By evening all was ready. Columbus had never been the type of sailor to become attached to the ships he sailed on, but this time he said a fond farewell to the *Nina*; the little ship had carried him safely across thousands of miles and through fierce storms.

As he stepped out of his cabin for the last time, Columbus gasped. Sailing down the river into the

port was the *Pinta*. She, too, had come home safely.

During Columbus's journey to Barcelona, messages went ahead of him and he soon found himself famous. In every town he was welcomed as a hero and people lined the streets or hung out of windows to cheer the great explorer and to stare at the Indians. Letters went to the far corners of Europe, telling of his voyage across the Atlantic and the islands he had discovered.

The excitement grew even higher as he entered the city of Barcelona. The streets were so crammed with cheering people that Columbus could hardly make his way to the castle where Isabella and Ferdinand waited. Ahead of him went six Indians wearing the golden jewellery of their people, squawking parrots, and a great pile of gold.

The hall of the Spanish King and Queen's castle was cool and quiet. Isabella and Ferdinand sat beneath a rich tapestry dressed in all the finery of court. As a show of respect for the Admiral, both of them stood as he entered and, when Columbus walked towards their thrones, the smiling Queen gave him her hand in welcome.

"My Lord Admiral," she said quietly as Columbus

kneeled before her. "We are grateful to God to see you returned safe and well. You have been successful, we hear."

"Your majesties," Columbus replied humbly, "I bring you word of lands I have discovered across the ocean sea; lands where the flag of Spain now flies. And I bring you gifts."

Clinking trays loaded with gold were brought forward at Columbus's signal and the Indians were pushed towards the king and queen, bowing as they had been taught.

Ferdinand permitted Columbus to stand. "So, these are our new people," the king said, looking with interest at the kneeling Indians. "Are there many of them?"

"They are countless in number, sire," said Columbus. "And they are strong, gentle folk who work well."

Seeing that Columbus meant that the Indians might be used as slaves, Isabella held out a hand. "No," she said. "It is our wish that they stay in their homes and be taught to worship God."

Columbus bowed his head.

"But come, Columbus," the Queen continued.

"Take a seat and tell us of your adventures,"

Some of the people in the hall gasped. To be asked to sit with the King and Queen was a great honour. For hours Columbus sat with the great sovereigns, their three heads almost touching as the Admiral pointed out his route and the lands he had found on a map. Then he spoke of the islands and their wonders, waving for samples of gold and plants, birds, and animals to be brought forward as he described them. These, he said, were just the beginning. There was much, much more left to find and all of it would bring great wealth to Spain.

As he finished his tale, both the King and the Queen fell to their knees and thanked God for bringing the new lands to Spain. After praying, Ferdinand looked at Columbus and said quietly, "You must make another voyage, and soon. Portugal already knows of your discoveries and word will spread. Many will want to take the lands you have found and we must make sure that they belong only to Spain."

"Do not fear, your majesty," replied Columbus. "I have kept the route very secret. Not even those who sailed with me would be able to find the way."

LIVESinACTION

Over the following weeks Columbus was showered with rewards. Isabella and Ferdinand judged that he was the winner of the prize they had promised to the first man to sight land, and he was also given his own coat of arms. Columbus was now a true nobleman. For days at a time he talked in secret with the King and Queen, giving them every last detail of his voyage and planning the next. He was also delighted to see Diego again and spent as much time as could be spared with his son. Eventually, however, preparations for the next voyage were at a point where the Admiral was needed at the port of Cadiz. This time, he would be in command of a fleet of seventeen ships loaded with more than 1,500 people. First though, he had a trip to make that he could not bear to put off any longer: to see Beatrix and his younger son Fernando.

For Columbus, these would be among the last happy days of his life. On the horizon, storm clouds were rolling in.

9
The Governor

"What happened here? For the love of God, someone tell me what happened here," hissed Columbus, his fists bunched in balls of anger.

The date was 28 November 1493, and Christopher Columbus stood on the island of Hispaniola with a group of soldiers and his brother Diego at his side. In front of him were the burned ruins of La Navidad fortress and the bodies of the men that he had left there in January. Not one of them was alive to answer his question.

Columbus's friend, the chieftain Guacanagari, had disappeared, too, along with most of the villagers, but over the next twenty-four hours a few Indians were found hiding among the trees. When they were questioned, the story unfolded. After the *Nina* had left, the men of La Navidad had begun fighting among themselves over gold and some had been killed. Later, the Spanish had become violent towards the peaceful Indians, dragging them off to be slaves and treating the women with terrible cruelty. The Indians had tried to stop them and more fighting had broken out. This time, the last of the Spanish men had died.

When he heard the tale Columbus's fury grew. He had hoped that the men of La Navidad would have collected a store of treasure in the ten months they had been on Hispaniola, which could be sent back to Spain to help pay for the seventeen expensive ships. Instead the fools had disobeyed his orders and died for it, leaving no gold for him.

On this new voyage his job was to build a town, of which he would be the governor with the power of the King and Queen in his hands. The destruction of La Navidad was a dreadful beginning. "We will leave a few men here," Columbus commanded, "but find a new site, a better place where we will build a city worthy of Spain."

Further to the east along the coast, Columbus picked out a spot for the new town, naming it Isabela. Even as animals and stores were being unloaded from the ships, the men whispered that the site was badly chosen. The sea was so shallow that ships were forced to anchor hundreds of yards away from the shore, making it difficult to get supplies onto land, and the closest stream for drinking water was over a mile away. Even worse, as the settlers would soon find out, there were swamps close by where disease-carrying insects lurked.

Soon, Isabela's new townsfolk began to fall sick and those who weren't too ill to speak complained bitterly about Columbus. After all that he had said back in Spain, the men who volunteered for the second voyage had expected to arrive at a paradise where gold could be picked up like pebbles from the ground. Instead, hundreds were ill, food was running out, there was little gold to be seen, and Columbus had put every man who wasn't too sick to building the new town, beginning with a church and a stone house for himself. Having set out from Spain as the famous navigator and the favourite of Isabella and Ferdinand, Columbus was now hated by the men he was supposed to command. Many of them talked openly about getting word to the

King and Queen about the town's suffering under its useless governor. A few even tried to steal two of the ships so that they could sail back to Spain.

By December, Columbus was sick too. Still, men came knocking at his door bringing him new complaints and new difficulties to solve. Shivering with fever, he found himself longing for the simple life at sea, a deck beneath his feet and the horizon ahead. As he recovered, Columbus decided to leave the worries of Isabela and take three ships on a new voyage.

Late in April 1494, feeling almost well again, Columbus gave command of Isabela over to Diego, and sailed out in search of new lands and riches. For five months his ships sailed along the coast of Cuba and then discovered the island of Jamaica, but Columbus found nothing to make the Spanish King and Queen rich, and eventually fell sick again. By the time he returned to Isabela in September 1494, he couldn't stand and his eyes were bleeding. It would be five months before Columbus had recovered enough to govern again. The only thing that gave him any reason to be cheerful was the arrival of his other brother, the quiet and faithful Bartholomew, from Spain. But soon after Bartholomew arrived, Columbus faced another disaster.

Diego Columbus had been an even worse governor of Isabela than his brother. While Columbus was away at sea, he had lost all control of the men under his command. The Spanish had caused chaos on the island, taking women and boys as slaves, and beating and killing Indians. As word of their cruelty spread, the Indians had banded together, determined to rid the island of the foreigners. Now, an army threatened to attack the small town.

On 24 March 1495, Columbus mounted a horse, trying not to let the pain he felt show on his face. On his order, 200 soldiers and twenty knights on horseback clattered through Isabela and out into the countryside. Ten miles from the little town, in a valley called Vega Real, the Spanish found more than 10,000 Indians ready to fight. With his face like stone, Columbus looked at the huge army of islanders, then back at his own tiny force. For every one Spanish soldier there were at least fifty of the Indians. He lifted his hand and yelled "Forward!"

LIVESinACTION

The Spanish tore the enemy army apart with ease. The Indians had only simple weapons and were no match for the Spanish guns, swords and vicious dogs. Soon, the valley echoed with screams of wounded and terrified Indians as they ran to hide. As he rode away from the horrifying battlefield, Columbus gritted his teeth in anger at the Indians and promised himself that such a battle would never be fought again. "From this day on," he told Diego and Bartholomew later that night, "I shall make this island and its people pay. We must get gold back to Spain."

Columbus was as good as his word. Although Queen Isabella had forbidden him to use the Indians as slaves, he ignored her orders and thousands were taken from their homes. In constant fear of terrible Spanish punishments, the people of Hispaniola were forced to serve their new masters. Desperate for gold, Columbus ordered that every Indian man, woman and child was to bring him a thimble full of the precious metal every three months. Those who failed to do so had one of their hands cut off. Month after month, the Indians of Hispaniola worked and died at the hands of the Spanish, and the gold they brought was never enough. Many ran away to hide in the mountains, and those who stayed found that their quiet, peaceful way of life had disappeared forever.

Meanwhile, the men of Isabela still complained about their hated governor and those who sailed home spread vicious gossip about Columbus's stupidity and the suffering he caused the Spanish settlers. None of them cared about the suffering of the Indians. Eventually, the gossip reached the ears of Isabella and Ferdinand. In order to clear his name, in March 1496, after two miserable years in the beautiful islands he had discovered, Columbus set sail for Spain again.

10

The Third Voyage

"Please stand Lord Admiral," said the Queen, touching Columbus on the shoulder.

Columbus looked up at her, surprise in his tired eyes. He knew that the King and Queen had not received as much gold as they had hoped for. He also knew that all the men who had returned from Hispaniola had brought with them tales of disease and suffering and had told anyone who would listen that he was a failure as governor. Columbus had expected the King and Queen to be angry, but while Ferdinand was colder than he had been before, Isabella was still warm and respectful.

It was true that his welcome had been very different: this time there had been no cheering crowds, and many people looked at him with scorn. As he looked up at the Queen's soft face, though,

Columbus did not care what anyone else thought.

"Your Majesty, there have been some problems on Hispaniola," he murmured. "The men do not like to work and the Indians have waged war on us. I have tried my best, and will do so again. A little more time is all that is needed…"

"We know you have done all that you can, my Lord, and we thank you for your efforts. If there is anything you need you have only to ask."

Columbus jumped at the chance offered by Isabella's unexpected generosity. "My queen," he said, "I have been thinking about a new voyage of discovery. So far I have found only islands but I am sure that the great lands of Asia are only a little further to the west."

"You shall have the ships you need, Columbus, and our blessings."

Despite Isabella's promise it was two years before Columbus sailed back across the Atlantic. Spain was at war with France, and Isabella was arranging marriages for her children. While the Queen's attention was on these important matters, the men who controlled the royal treasury did whatever they could to delay Columbus. Every expense was argued over and obstacles put in his path so that he was forced to wait month after slow month for his new ships.

While he waited, two other sailors set out on voyages that would become almost as famous as Columbus's. In the summer of 1497, an Italian navigator called John Cabot sailed across the Atlantic, far to the north, and found lands that would later become parts of Canada and the United States of America. Around the same time, the Portuguese navigator Vasco da Gama set out from Lisbon on a voyage around Africa and discovered a route to the real Asia. He landed in India on 20 May 1498, and his discovery brought Portugal the wealth that Columbus had dreamed of winning for Spain.

Columbus knew nothing of this, however, and waited with growing impatience for the six ships he was to take across the Atlantic. Finally, on 30 May 1498, he left the port of Sanlucar in southern Spain. Now almost 47 years old, Columbus's face was wrinkled from his years of trouble and he had grown a long beard. His illness had left him weak and in constant pain from stiff joints and swollen feet; his eyes were bad and his mind sometimes wandered. But he was still determined to find what he had been seeking for so long.

After a little over two months at sea, on 5 August Columbus looked over the rail of his ship at what he thought must be another island in the distance. Three of his six ships had been sent towards Hispaniola with urgent supplies and he was now hundreds of miles to the south east with the remaining three. Four days earlier, they had come to a large island that Columbus had named Trinidad, but seeing little of interest there they had sailed on to the west.

Over the following days, Columbus stopped several times on the shore of this new land and learned from the Indians who lived there that it was called Paria. Not guessing that he and his crew were the first Europeans to see what is now Venezuela, at the north east of the continent of South America, Columbus was most excited to find that the local people wore jewellery decorated with valuable pearls. Like the Indians Columbus had first met on Hispaniola, these folk happily gave their treasures away for the price of a few beads and told him that more pearls could be found further to the west.

As the ships sailed on, Columbus began to be puzzled by the great, flat land they were passing. It did not look like any island he had so far discovered but stretched away to the far horizon. For mile after mile the three tiny ships followed its coastline and as each day passed Columbus grew more certain that he had found a continent. Forgetting to sleep and gazing out over the rail until his eyes began to bleed again, he watched as the coast passed by.

On 12 August, a ship's boy called out to him in a confused voice, "Lord Admiral, there's something wrong with the water here."

"What is it?" Columbus asked impatiently.

"Taste it," the boy answered bringing a bucket over the side of the ship and offering it to Columbus.

The admiral dipped his hand in and sipped at the seawater. It should have been salty and undrinkable but it tasted almost as fresh as if it had come from a mountain spring.

"A river," Columbus muttered, glancing at the coastline. "We must be close to the mouth of a very great river, but if this is an island that doesn't make sense."

"What do you mean, Admiral?" asked the boy.

"The sea is always salty," Columbus said. "Except where the fresh water of a river pours into it, and this far out at sea it would have to be an enormous river to make the water fresh."

"Why is a river so special, Admiral? We have seen lots of them."

"Don't you see boy? No island would have a river of this size. The land would have to be vast. A continent. Like... like Asia."

For as long as the sun was in the sky, Columbus stayed on deck watching for sight of the great river that would prove him right. The next day, 13 August 1498, the ships arrived at one of the branches of the Orinoco River, the second largest in South America. It was proof that the land Columbus had found was part of a great continent. Still, he was puzzled. None of the charts he had ever seen showed a continent this far to the south. Surely there was no such thing as a whole continent missing from the map of the world? Checking again and again, Columbus attempted to solve the problem, trying to fit the continent into his maps. He failed every time. The only way he could explain it was if Paria was a land that no-one had ever heard of or seen before.

That night, Columbus began a letter to Isabella and Ferdinand that would take him days to finish. It was long and rambling, full of descriptions of the new continent, but sleepless nights and illness made his mind wander in strange directions. As he told the King and Queen about Paria, he began to believe that it was the Garden of Eden where God had made Adam and Eve.

While Columbus scribbled page after page, the ships sailed on along the coast until, a few days after the ship had left the Orinoco behind, it was obvious that the Admiral was seriously ill. The captains of the other two ships came aboard to tell him that they were worried about his health and that the supplies they were carrying for Hispaniola were beginning to go rotten. Columbus gave new orders. On 22 August, just three weeks after Trinidad had been found, the three ships turned to the north and headed towards Hispaniola.

11

Columbus in Chains

It had been more than two years since Columbus had left Hispaniola. When he arrived there at the end of August he found that Bartholomew and Diego had abandoned the little town of Isabela and ordered a new one to be built. Called Santo Domingo, it was on the south eastern coast of the island and had a church, governor's mansion, and smaller houses for the Spanish settlers. Santo Domingo's river provided a safe harbour close to the shore and gave the townsfolk as much fresh water as they needed.

Little else had changed. Under Columbus's two brothers, the situation on Hispaniola was as bad as he had left it, or worse. The Spanish hated Bartholomew and Diego as much as Columbus himself and made as much trouble on the island as they could. The Indians were treated with terrible brutality and they, too, often rebelled.

They were also suffering another torment. The Spanish had brought with them from Europe diseases that had never touched the island before; diseases that spread quickly among the Indian people and from which they never recovered. Hundreds of thousands had died and rather than trying to help their neighbours, the Spanish complained that there weren't enough Indians left to work their farms and mines.

For weeks Columbus remained sick and weak, but as his strength returned he did all he could to ignore the problems of Hispaniola. Occasionally, he took some of the few men still loyal to him and attacked a group of Spanish or Indian rebels, bringing them back to Santo Domingo to be hanged, but mostly he concentrated on working his own lands. He sent the letter describing the new continent as the Garden of Eden back to Isabella and Ferdinand though, on a ship that returned to Spain in October, 1498.

Unfortunately for him, word of his sensational discovery was not the only news the ship carried.

Also aboard were angry letters from the Spaniards of Hispaniola, men who were eager to spread word of Bartholomew, Diego and Christopher Columbus's failings, of the diseases that were killing the Spanish, the hunger, and the hangings of those who spoke out against the brothers.

The ship reached Spain early in 1500 and this time Isabella and Ferdinand could no longer turn a blind eye. Shortly after its arrival, they picked a man called Francisco de Bobadillo to sail across the Atlantic and take command of Hispaniola.

While the ship carrying his letter was still crossing Atlantic waves, in December 1499, though, the governor finally received news to lift his spirits.

"How much?" he asked a Spanish man in ragged clothes who stood before him with his head bowed.

"More than you can imagine," came the reply. "We are already digging a new mine, and there is more than I have ever seen before."

"This is good," whispered Columbus, his eyes ablaze with greed. "Very good. At last this island begins to pay."

On the table in front of him was a pile of freshly mined gold. Eighty miles to the north west of

Santo Domingo, just beneath the surface of the hills, there was so much of the precious metal that any man could easily find more in one day than he might earn in a year as a sailor.

For months, the Spanish and their Indian slaves mined great quantities of gold while Columbus waited impatiently for ships that might carry the good news back to Spain. When they arrived, however, they carried a passenger who brought disaster for Columbus.

On 23 August 1500, Francisco de Bobadillo stepped onto the shore at Santo Domingo. He was greeted by the sight of seven dead Spanish rebels hanging by their necks in the centre of the town.

"What is the meaning of this?" de Bobadillo roared at Diego as he walked into the governor's mansion. "Why are good Spanish men hanging in your square? And where is Governor Columbus?"

"Those men were rebels who plotted to overthrow the Governor," replied Diego coldly. "Both my brothers are at this very moment riding against more of their kind. And who, sir, are you?"

De Bobadillo threw some papers onto the desk in front of Diego. "If you read these, sir," he sneered, "you will find that I am the new Governor of these islands: sent by their majesties to bring order where you and your brothers have only brought misery."

Diego's face went white as he took the papers in shaking hands. De Bobadillo leaned over until his face was just a foot from Diego's. "That's right," he whispered. "Your brother has been removed from his post by order of the King and Queen, and after what I have seen here today, I'll make sure all three of you are sent back to Spain in chains."

De Bobadillo called in men who pulled Diego roughly from his chair. Within minutes, he had been thrown into Santo Domingo's jail while the new governor sent riders to fetch Christopher and Bartholomew Columbus.

Three weeks later, the three brothers stood on trial before de Bobadillo, surrounded by the Spanish men of Hispaniola. Hundreds had come to tell the new governor how difficult life had been on the island. One after another, they spoke of how they had starved under Columbus; how he had ignored their problems and looked only to make himself rich; how he had treated those who disagreed with him brutally. Some of them spoke the truth. Many more told lies to blacken his name.

At the end of the trial, de Bobadillo got out of his chair. In a stern voice, he declared, "Christopher Columbus, I have heard enough that I can reach only one decision. These islands were given to you by the King and the Queen to rule in their name, and you have failed utterly. Not only that, but you have caused great suffering among the people and put your own greed before their health. My decision is this: I am taking from you all the lands you own here and sending you to Spain, where you will stand trial before their majesties. For your crimes, I hope you and your brothers spend the rest of your lives in prison."

While the crowd cheered and jeered, Christopher, Diego, and Bartholomew Columbus were loaded with chains until they could hardly walk. Then they were led away to the harbour where ships waited to take them across the Atlantic.

Christopher Columbus's third voyage was at an end. At the end of October 1500, he began the long journey back to Spain. Once he had returned as a hero, but now he was carried as a prisoner.

12

The High Voyage

Throughout the long journey back to Spain, the ship's captain tried to persuade Columbus to let him take off the heavy chains. Every time, Columbus replied that he would only take them off when Isabella and Ferdinand ordered it. Sunk in gloom, chains rattling on his wrists painfully, he wrote a long letter to the King and Queen complaining of his treatment, and telling them of the new continent he had found and the gold that was being dug up on Hispaniola.

When the ship reached the port of Cadiz, Columbus was taken to a monastery close by and for five weeks remained a prisoner there. In December a letter arrived. Shaking with relief, Columbus read the Queen's words over and over: "We were very upset by news of your imprisonment," Isabella had written. "As soon as we heard, we sent orders for you to be released." The letter went on to order Columbus to come to court where Ferdinand and Isabella wished to see him.

Once again, Columbus kneeled and looked up into the Queen's soft face. "We are sorry for your sufferings, my Lord," she said gently. "We did not expect de Bobadillo to go so far."

"Then you will give me back all that he has taken from me?" asked Columbus hopefully. "Will you send me back to Hispaniola as Governor? My lands will be returned?"

"We will look into returning your lands, but you must not return to Hispaniola. If you go back, the people will make great trouble for you and for me. My hope is that de Bobadillo brings peace to the island."

"But I have brought you gold, a new continent..."

Unknown to Columbus, after reading his earlier letter about Paria, Isabella and Ferdinand had sent out four navigators to find out if what he said was true. Every one of them had returned with the news that Columbus had, indeed, discovered a land that could not be found on any map. They had also brought back pearls and gold. De Bobadillo, too, had sent word that a vast amount of gold had been found on Hispaniola. It was this news that had made Isabella and Ferdinand decide to treat Columbus with kindness. But now that Hispaniola was producing gold, the last thing the King and Queen wanted was more trouble on the island.

"We will see what can be done," Isabella continued. "But you have been far away for two years. Take some rest. Spend some time with Beatrix and your sons and try to forget about all that has happened."

Columbus did not forget though. Over the next two years he wrote to the Queen demanding more of Hispaniola's riches. As the months passed, he also began to plan for a new voyage – his "high voyage". The last, Columbus decided, had been too short. This time, he wanted to see how big the new continent he had discovered was, and, of course, to find what riches it held.

When he asked Isabella and Ferdinand to give him ships, in February 1502, they quickly agreed, and four caravels were ready within weeks. Isabella and Ferdinand were quietly glad that Columbus would be far away from court and they might have some peace from his endless requests. Everything was arranged as Columbus asked, and the King and Queen asked only one thing in return. On this voyage Columbus was forbidden to go near Hispaniola.

On 9 May, Columbus sailed out of Cadiz, with his thirteen-year-old son Fernando on board as well as his brother Bartholomew. Columbus was now fifty-one, an old man, and sickness, worry, and trouble had made him look even older. His eyes were failing and the pain in his feet and joints meant that even walking a few steps was agony.

The four ships crossed the Atlantic in calm seas and Columbus was sailing dangerously close to the forbidden island of Hispaniola when he saw the black clouds of a storm blowing across the horizon. He had been sailing around the islands for long enough to know that a gale of the sort the Indians called a 'hurrican' was blowing up and that the caravels would be in terrible danger.

"Head for shore," he cried in a shaking voice. "We have to find shelter or we'll be sunk. Make for Santo Domingo."

But when Hispaniola's new governor, Ovando, found out that Columbus was aboard one of the ships that had come to find shelter, he ordered the caravels to leave immediately. Columbus was forced to take his ships back out into the growing storm and find shelter further along the coast.

The worst of the hurricane was avoided, but for the next month bitter winds blew around the struggling vessels while they sailed slowly around Jamaica and then north to the coast of Cuba. From there, Columbus was chased by the storm as the caravels headed west towards the great continent he had come to explore.

At last, on 14 August, they reached the shore of what is now known as Central America – the narrow strip of land that connects North and South America.

For the next nine months, Columbus led his small fleet south along 1,800 miles of coast. Storm after storm battered the caravels and progress was slow. Columbus found gold and pearls, but no cities and no mines as rich as those he had left on Hispaniola. Those discoveries would have to wait for later explorers.

Instead, he discovered more trouble. Old, in pain, and eager to see what lay ahead, Columbus forgot about cleaning and repairing the ships properly and as they sailed onwards they fell into terrible condition. One was abandoned during an attack by Indians. Another was later left behind when it became too rotten to sail any further. On 16 April 1503, afraid that his last two ships could not stay afloat much longer, Columbus gave the order to sail north for Hispaniola. A little over a month later, the caravels were caught in yet another storm and, this time, they were in no state to sail through it. Desperate that the ships should not sink at sea where everyone aboard would be drowned, the crew sailed both caravels through fierce waves straight onto a beach on the island of Jamaica then threw themselves ashore, thankful to be alive.

With both ships broken beyond repair, Columbus and his crew were stranded. One brave sailor, Diego Mendez, was given a canoe by the islanders which he managed to sail to Hispaniola, but for months Ovando would not let him into the town. It was June, 1504, almost a year after he had been stranded on Jamaica, that Columbus saw

Mendez return in a small ship he had managed to hire. During that time the Indians of Jamaica had helped the sailors survive, giving them food and shelter. Nevertheless, there had been many fights among the Spanish and against the Indians.

For the last time, Columbus sailed across the Atlantic and arrived back in Sanlucar on 7 November. With all four of his caravels wrecked and many men dead, his 'high' voyage was at a tragic end, though in years to come other Spaniards would revisit the new lands he had found. They would discover great cities built around pyramids and, a little way to the west, across the narrow strip of Central America, another ocean; an ocean which, if crossed, brought a ship to the eastern shores of Asia, just as Columbus had said.

Epilogue

Three weeks after Columbus landed in Sanlucar, Queen Isabella died. She had been Columbus's great champion at the Spanish court and had always listened to him. Now she was gone, Columbus was ignored, except for a single short meeting with King Ferdinand in early 1506.

After he had seen the king, Columbus retired to a house in the Spanish town of Valladolid. He was old and sick but by now he was a wealthy man. Even so, the last months of his life were miserable. Columbus had discovered more than he ever could have dreamed of as a young boy in Genoa but he had never found the golden cities of Asia and his fame had faded since the glorious return from the first voyage. No-one spoke of him and few seemed to remember who had discovered Spain's golden islands across the seas. On 20 May 1506, after many years of illness, Christopher Columbus died, with his sons and faithful Bartholomew at his bedside.

After his death, however, Columbus's name began to grow more famous than he could ever have imagined. Where Columbus had first set foot, other Spanish explorers followed, bringing back tales of cities and gold. To the north, sailors from other parts of Europe had begun mapping a shoreline that was just as vast. Soon, all of Europe understood that what Columbus had found was not the edge of Asia but a completely unknown place. Eventually, ships would sail around the tip of South America and into the Pacific Ocean and maps would be made that joined up the new coastlines to show not one but two vast continents. As Columbus died a different name for it was already being used: his discovery was called the 'New World'. Within a few decades, new European settlements could be found along the shores of the New World and some people had already started marking it on maps under yet another name: America.

The voyages of Christopher Columbus changed the world forever. Over the following centuries the continents were divided up into what would become powerful nations. For the people who lived on the lands he discovered, though, the change came at a terrible price. When Columbus first landed on Hispaniola and become friends with Guacanagari, the Indians who lived on the island called themselves 'Tainos'. We don't know how many Tainos there were: many people think the population was around a million, though some suggest it was up to eight million. But we do know that, twenty years later, only a few thousand Tainos were left. Most had died of the diseases the Spanish brought with them but many had been worked to death or murdered by their new masters. After another few years the Tainos of Hispaniola were gone completely.

As Europeans moved into America, a similar story would be repeated everywhere across the two continents. People whose ancestors had lived in America for thousands of years died of the diseases that came with the Europeans, or they were forced off their homelands to make room for the new settlers. Many more were enslaved or killed in wars as they tried to defend their homes. And as the Europeans spread, the land itself changed, too. Great forests were cut down to provide wood and to make way for farms while birds and animals were hunted until they were gone forever.

As more and more people sailed across the Atlantic to find new lands, adventures, and riches in the New World, Columbus's name became more famous. His son Fernando wrote of his father's great voyages of discovery and soon so did many other writers and poets. Eventually, American lands that Columbus had never seen or even known existed were named after him and statues erected to his memory. Christopher Columbus was the man who had discovered America, and years after he died, every school child there, and around the world, would learn of his adventures.

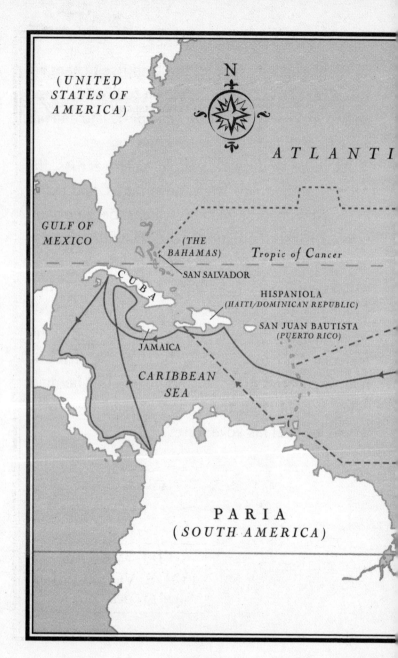

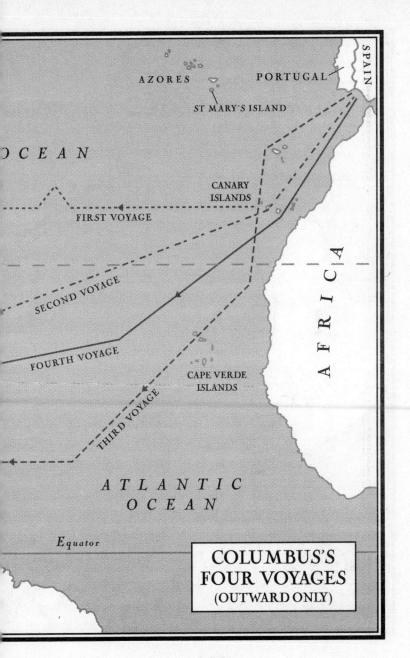

AZORES

PORTUGAL

SPAIN

ST MARY'S ISLAND

OCEAN

CANARY
ISLANDS

FIRST VOYAGE

AFRICA

SECOND VOYAGE

FOURTH VOYAGE

CAPE VERDE
ISLANDS

THIRD VOYAGE

ATLANTIC
OCEAN

Equator

**COLUMBUS'S
FOUR VOYAGES
(OUTWARD ONLY)**

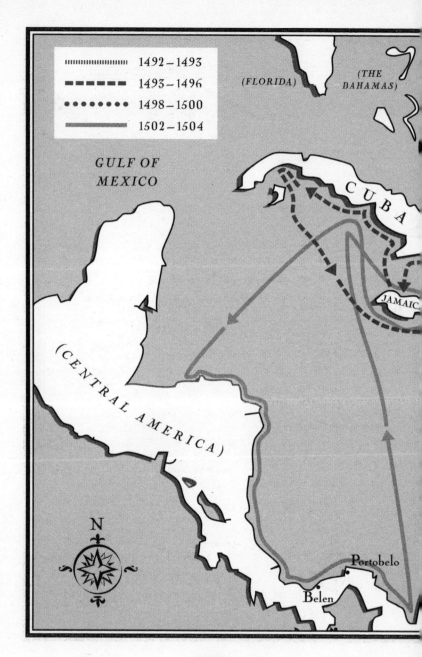

(symbol)	1492–1493
(symbol)	1493–1496
(symbol)	1498–1500
(symbol)	1502–1504

(FLORIDA)

(THE BAHAMAS)

GULF OF MEXICO

C U B A

JAMAIC

(CENTRAL AMERICA)

N

Portobelo

Belen

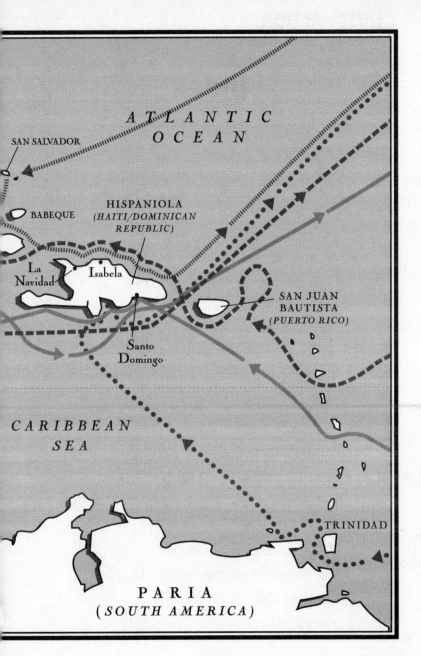

ATLANTIC
OCEAN

SAN SALVADOR

BABEQUE

HISPANIOLA
(HAITI/DOMINICAN
REPUBLIC)

La
Navidad   Isabela

SAN JUAN
BAUTISTA
(PUERTO RICO)

Santo
Domingo

CARIBBEAN
SEA

TRINIDAD

PARIA
(SOUTH AMERICA)

Index

LIVESinACTION